Hardie Grant acknowledges the Traditional Owners of the Country on which we work, the Wurundjeri People of the Kulin Nation and the Gadigal People of the Eora Nation, and recognises their continuing connection to the land, waters and culture. We pay our respects to their Elders past and present.

Wildling Books
Hardie Grant Children's Publishing
Wurundjeri Country
Level 11, 36 Wellington Street
Collingwood Victoria 3066
Melbourne | Sydney | San Francisco

hardiegrant.com/childrens

ISBN: 9781761214707
First published in Australia in 2025

A catalogue record for this book is available from the National Library of Australia

Printed and bound in HeShan China, November 2025
by LEO Paper Products LTD.

The paper this book is printed on is from FSC® certified forests and other controlled sources. FSC® promotes environmentally responsible, socially beneficial and economically viable management of the world's forests.

2 4 6 5 3

LET IT GO

REBEKAH LIPP · CRAIG PHILLIPS

When feelings arise –

even BIG ones, you'll find

They'll come and then go

they'll **FLOW** like a tide.

Fear could come calling

Or rage might stop by

You'll be visited by sadness

Sit with shame for a while.

There are **LESSONS** in feelings –

even big ones, you know

They are there to be felt

they'll help you to **GROW**.

Some days you'll feel sad

with a heart weighing **HEAVY**

Maybe welled with despair

or left feeling empty.

All alone, lost in sorrow

a gloom you can't shake

Just remember this trick

to **LIFT** the heartache …

Close your eyes. Let the sadness
drift high and pass by

Set it sailing on a breath-filled

clear midnight sky.

Feelings are just **ENERGY** in motion

and so …

When it's time, you'll know –

to let go, let them **FLOW**.

Now and then you'll feel **ANGER**

with a belly full of fire!

Fanned into temper

or boiled-over in ire.

Swept up in a storm

too **FIERCE** to be tamed

Just remember this trick

to help the fires wane …

BREATHE deep, so that fire inside

cools to stone

Hurl it hard across oceans

let it sink into calm.

Feelings are just **ENERGY** in motion,

and so …

When it's time, you'll know –

– to let go, let them **FLOW**.

You might feel shame

from what you said, did – or felt!

Or you'll shrink – **HIDE AWAY** –
from the blame you've been dealt.

When wound up in **WORRY**

from a careless misstep

Just remember this trick

to let go the regret …

Take the shame, write it down

then fold it up tight

Let broad paper wings

bear the weight and take flight.

Feelings are just **ENERGY** in motion,

and so …

When it's time, you'll know –

to let go, let them **FLOW**.

You'll be **AFRAID** sometimes
maybe frozen with dread

Aghast at the thought
of **MISFORTUNE** ahead.

Or a towering **FRIGHT**

that quickens your heart

Just remember this trick

to ward off the dark …

Make **FRIENDS** with the fear

hear its message for you

It'll call you to COURAGE
or help guide you through.

Because feelings are just **ENERGY** in motion

you know …

They are there to be felt –

they'll help you to GROW!

THE WORD EMOTION COMES FROM *EMOTERE*, WHICH MEANS 'ENERGY IN MOTION' IN LATIN!

Throughout this book, Aroha and her friends each experience an emotion and find a unique way to release that energy from their body. You will notice the golden line of energy moving throughout the pages. This represents the energy in motion or the emotion as it starts and ends with each child.

OLLIE EXPERIENCES SADNESS

Have you ever felt really sad before? Ollie imagines blowing out his sadness and filling up lots of hot-air lanterns – so many that it fills the night sky. His sadness is transformed into something beautiful and it makes him feel happier. Crying is the body's way to release some sadness. Always allow yourself, and others, space to cry if needed. What other ways can you think of to release sadness?

AROHA IS VISITED BY ANGER

Have you ever felt really angry before? Aroha knows to breathe deep when anger visits. She imagines her anger turning into little stones that she can drop into cool water. What ways can you think of to release anger in a safe way? Maybe you could try moving your body by doing star jumps. What about an 'anger pillow' that you can yell into or bang on your bed to release the emotion?

CHARLIE HAS TO DEAL WITH A VERY UNCOMFORTABLE EMOTION ... SHAME

We all experience being ashamed or feeling shame at some time. Charlie finds that writing down her feelings and making them into paper planes then throwing away that discomfort makes her feel better. She then writes down things that make her feel happy or lists things she is good at. If you feel you can't talk about your feelings, maybe you could try writing them down and giving the note to someone you trust. What other ways can you think of to release shame?

MASON EXPERIENCES FEAR

Have you ever felt really scared before? Mason understands that his fear is trying to protect him, so he imagines making friends with it. He imagines talking with his fear and as he does, the fear gets smaller and less scary. What ways can you think of to release fear?

PARENT/TEACHER NOTES

Hold space for your children to feel and do the same for yourself. Create a quiet, safe space for when big emotions come to visit. Remember, a child's behaviour is a form of communication. What we can do as parents/teachers/caregivers is show our children healthy and safe ways to express their emotions without suppressing them. Let children know that you are there to support them by saying, 'I am here'.

It is really important to learn healthy ways to release emotions so we don't store unwanted emotions in our body. Always make sure that you, and those around you, are safe when you do it. Sometimes when we feel a strong uncomfortable emotion, if we are mindful, we can feel parts of our body getting tight or contracting. Look back through the pages and see how often the children's bodies are curled up with their feelings. Notice that after they find a way to release that energy their bodies expand back into fullness again.

HOW TO PROCESS EMOTIONS WITHIN THE BODY:

NOTICE THE EMOTION AND WHERE YOU CAN FEEL IT IN YOUR BODY.

LABEL THE EMOTION. 'THIS IS SADNESS' OR 'THIS IS FEAR'.

ALLOW YOUR EMOTIONS SPACE AND ACKNOWLEDGE THEY ARE WITH YOU.

ALWAYS REMEMBER THAT ALL EMOTIONS WILL PASS. GIVE IT TIME.

THINK ABOUT WHAT COULD HAVE HAPPENED FOR THE EMOTION TO VISIT YOU.

WHEN YOU FEEL READY, LET THE EMOTION GO IN A WAY THAT WORKS FOR YOU.

Remind children they are not their emotions. Instead of saying, 'I am angry,' try saying, 'I am feeling angry' or 'This is anger visiting me'. No emotion is 'good' or 'bad'. All emotions serve a purpose and it is healthy to experience a broad range of emotions. Learning to recognise and label our emotions is really useful. Give children the language to use. For example, if they look frustrated, ask them, 'Are you feeling frustrated right now?' Let children know they can ask for help if they feel their emotions are hard to control or are upsetting them.

Work out which way works best for your child to LET IT GO!

MORE WILDLING BOOKS!

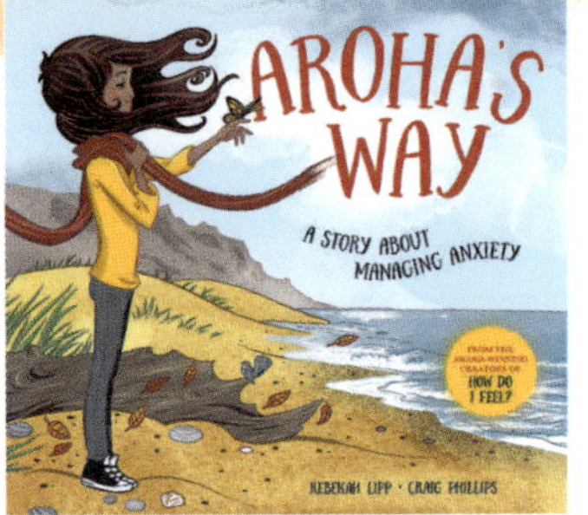

AROHA'S WAY

A story about managing anxiety.

AROHA KNOWS

A story about the calming power of nature.

AROHA'S CHOICE

A story about the impact of positive thoughts.

HOW DO I FEEL?

An essential emotional literacy tool for children with 60+ definitions inside!

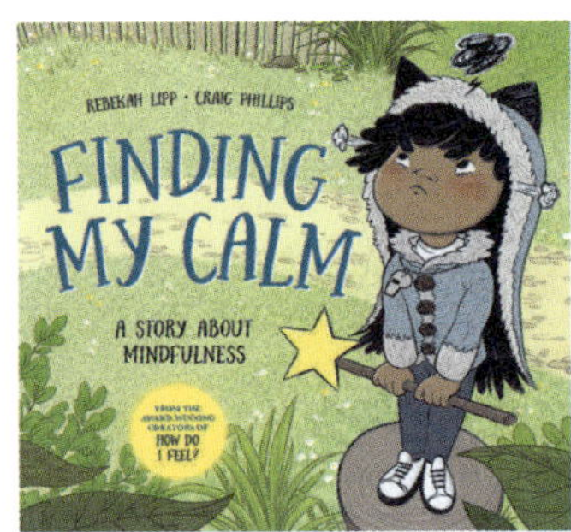

FINDING MY CALM

A story about mindfulness.

LET IT GO

A story about navigating big emotions.

BIG EMOTIONS FOR LITTLE PEOPLE

The perfect introduction to emotions big and small!

LET IT FLOW

A guide to healthy emotional expression for children.